The DBA's Guide

to

SharePoint 2013

STEVEN MANN

The DBA's Guide to SharePoint 2013

Copyright © 2013 by Steven Mann

Trademarks

Screenshots of Microsoft Products and Services

Warning and Disclaimer

Cover By: David H. Ross (http://davidhross.com/)

Dedication

To my two favorite DBAs Biju Samuel and Baur Smagulov

Acknowledgement

Special thanks to Todd Klindt for allowing me to use one of his PowerShell solutions.

Table of Contents

This page intentionally blank

Introduction

This book explores database management of SharePoint 2013. SharePoint 2013 may be installed and configured using either SQL Server 2008 R2 or SQL Server 2012. Many times SharePoint Administrators and SharePoint Developers overlook SQL Server in a SharePoint environment. It is there, it functions, and it's a black-box to many. SQL Server is essential to a productive SharePoint farm as that's where 90% of the content, configurations, settings, etc. are stored. Without SQL Server, there is no SharePoint.

Therefore, this book dives into the various databases, discusses best practices, and outlines tactical operations. A perfect reference for SQL Server DBAs and SharePoint Administrators that have authority over SQL Server in a SharePoint farm.

Stay updated with my blog posts: www.SteveTheManMann.com

This page intentionally blank

CHAPTER 1

Database Overview

This chapter introduces the various types of databases within a SharePoint farm and explores each type and instance.

Types of SharePoint Databases

The databases that are created for use of SharePoint 2013 are categorized as one of three types:

- Configuration
- Content
- Service Application

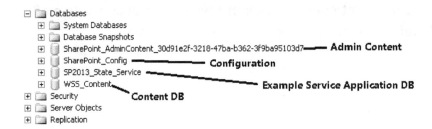

The configuration database is created when you install the first instance of SharePoint and create a new farm. There is only one configuration database and it is essentially your "farm" from a SQL Server perspective. When you attach servers to your farm you select the configuration database accordingly. The Central Administration content database may also be considered a configuration database as the content it stores deals with the configuration of the farm. More details about the configuration database are explained in the next section.

Not to sound smart but the content databases store all of the content within the SharePoint sites. Each Web Application that is created on the farm may have one or more content databases associated. This is where all of the pages, list items, documents, etc. are physically stored. The smallest block of content in a content database is a site collection. Therefore, a content database stores one or more site collections. A sit e collection can only "live" in one content database.

It is a good idea to have multiple content databases to help partition the SharePoint sites and provide flexibility in backup and restoring. It is much easier to maintain a 40GB database than a 400GB database for example. This book will explain more details and functions that may be performed with content databases.

Finally, the DBA's nightmare, are the service application databases. For each service application in SharePoint, one or more databases are created to maintain the settings and configurations of the particular service application.

Previously in SharePoint 2007 (MOSS 2007), several of these services (Search, User Profiles, Business Data Catalog, and Excel Services) were combined into the Shared Service Provider (SSP) service of SharePoint. Usually this meant only one SSP database although you could have more than one SSP and thus multiple databases.

SharePoint 2010 changed the architecture of the SSP and split out each service into its own service application. This provided more flexibility and scalability; however, it also created more databases.

The same architecture model exists in SharePoint 2013 and there are several new service applications - which again means more databases. So that's why I say these are the DBA's nightmares because now there can be 10-20 databases just for the service applications (Enterprise search creates and uses four itself). Each service application database is explained in a future section of this chapter.

Configuration Database

```
☐ 📁 Databases
   ⊞ 📁 System Databases
   ⊞ 📁 Database Snapshots
   ⊞ 📁 SharePoint_AdminContent_30d91e2f-3218-47ba-b362-3f9ba95103d7
   ⊞ 📁 SharePoint_Config
   ⊞ 📁 SP2013_State_Service
   ⊞ 📁 WSS_Content
⊞ 📁 Security
⊞ 📁 Server Objects
⊞ 📁 Replication
⊞ 📁 AlwaysOn High Availability
⊞ 📁 Management
```

The configuration database, as explained previously, is essentially the "farm" from a SQL Server perspective. This database is generally small and should maintain with less than 1GB of space.

The configuration database stores data about the following:

- All of the other SharePoint databases

- IIS Web Sites

- Site Templates

- Specific Farm Settings - Quotas, Blocked File Types

- Trusted Solutions

- Web Applications

- Web Part Packages

This database is very read intensive, however, as modifications and deployments are executed, the transaction logs can get bloated. Therefore if you keep the recovery model in the default

Full state, it is recommended to backup the transaction log regularly for truncation purposes. Otherwise, it is recommended to switch the recovery model of the configuration database to Simple.

Central Administration Content Database

```
⊞ 📁 System Databases
⊞ 📁 Database Snapshots
⊞ 📄 SharePoint_AdminContent_30d91e2f-3218-47ba-b362-3f9ba95103d7
⊞ 📄 SharePoint_Config
⊞ 📄 SP2013_State_Service
⊞ 📄 WSS_Content
```

The Central Administration (Central Admin) Content Database is used store the content of the Central Admin web application which is used to administer and configure farm wide systems and services. This database also is generally small and should maintain at less than 1GB of disk space (just like the configuration database). The recovery model defaults to Full it is fine to keep it that way. There shouldn't be too much read/writes as it is usually just the SharePoint Administrator(s) who is/are making modifications and generally content such as documents is not uploaded to Central Admin like a normal content database.

However, it could increase in size if PowerPivot is installed and deployed within the SharePoint farm. All of the Excel worksheets and Power Pivot data files used in the Power Pivot Management Dashboard are stored within the Central Admin content database.

The default database name is SharePoint_AdminContent_<guid>. DBA's tend to hate the GUID in the database name because a) it is not "clean" and b) backup programs tend to have issues with the GUID involved. Therefore it is recommended to create the Central Admin site via PowerShell as explained in Chapter 2.

Content Databases

```
☐ 🗀 Databases
    ☐ 🗀 System Databases
    ☐ 🗀 Database Snapshots
    ☐ 🗀 SharePoint_AdminContent_30d91e2f-3218-47ba-b362-3f9ba95103d7
    ☐ 🗀 SharePoint_Config
    ☐ 🗀 SP2013_State_Service
    ☐ 🗀 WSS_Content
☐ 🗀 Security
☐ 🗀 Server Objects
```

The Content Databases store all of the content for all of the site collections on the farm within a given web application. This includes list items, documents, web part settings, user information, and other site related configurations.

Each web application must have at least one content database but may have multiple. A site collection can only live in one content database. While the recommended max size is 200GB (although up to 1TB is supported), I personally like smaller 40-50GB content databases. It is easier to backup and restore smaller databases as well as copying the backup files around to different servers.

Web Application

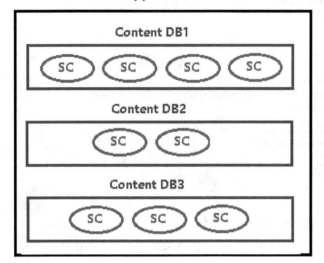

Service Application Databases

The service application databases are created when their respective service applications are created. If not all service applications are needed or created, then obviously the databases are not needed or created.

App Management Database

The App Management database is used by the App Management Service Application. It is used to store configurations and license information for Apps installed on the SharePoint farm.

This database should remain fairly small taking up less than 1GB of space with a default recovery model of Full.

Business Data Connectivity Service Database

The Business Data Connectivity Service database services the Business Data Connectivity Service Application. This service application is often referred to BDC or BCS. BCS is the updated term.

Since this database stores external content types, it is very read intensive. However, this database should remain fairly small taking up less than 1GB of space with a default recovery model of Full.

Managed Metadata Service Database

The Managed Metadata Service database is used to store the taxonomies and term sets maintained within the Managed Metadata Service Application. This database should stay below 100GB or even smaller depending on the amount of metadata is being used within the SharePoint farm.

Machine Translation Service Database

This database is used for the Machine Translation Service Application. It should remain fairly small and defaults to Full recovery.

Project Server Database

This database is used for the Project Web Application. It should remain fairly small and defaults to Full recovery.

Power Pivot Database

This database is used for Power Pivot. It should remain fairly small and defaults to Full recovery.

PerformancePoint Services Database

This database is used for PerformancePoint Services Service Application. It should remain fairly small and defaults to Full recovery.

Search Service Application Databases

There are several databases that are needed to support the Search Service Application.

Search Administration Database

This database is the core Search Service Application database and is usually named without the "admin" suffix. It has a simple recovery model by default and stores all of the main search administration settings including but not limited to, content sources, result sources, and query rules. This database can grow to a decent size if Search is used well in your SharePoint farm; plan on it getting as large as 50-100GB. This database has a default recovery mode of Simple.

Search Analytics Reporting Database

The Search Analytics Reporting database maintains metrics from all of the search activity (queries, retrievals,etc.) and is updated by a nightly timer job process. Depending on search usage this database can grow very large easily reaching 100GB+.

It is recommended to scale out this database using a split operation if and when the database size grows past 200GB.

Search Crawl Database

The Search Crawl database maintains crawl information from all of the search crawling of the active content sources and is updated by full and incremental crawls. Depending on the searchable content, this database can grow up to 100GB.

It is recommended to scale out this database by creating new search crawl databases for each 20 million search items.

Search Link Database

After items are crawled, content processing actually gathers the information and performs indexing of the content. The links from this content processing are stored within the Search Link database. When users click a search result item link, the click-through action is also recorded in the Search Link database.

Therefore, this database can grow fairly large based on both the amount of searchable content as well as the number of queries executed by SharePoint users. During content processing there will be more intensive write activity - although the default recovery model is Simple.

It is recommended to scale this database out by adding another Search Link database for every sixty million documents crawled and for every 100 million queries expected per year.

Secure Store Database

The Secure Store Database is used by the Secure Store Service and stores configured credentials for external systems/applications. Since this data is very small, the size of this database should remain small as well. It is not expected that this database would grow past 1GB with most instances maintaining less than 100MB. The default recovery model is Full.

State Service Database

The State Service database is used to store Session State service in SharePoint. It can become fairly large depending on the usage of features that utilize session state. It defaults to a Full recovery model.

Usage and Health Database

The Usage and Health Collection database can and will become a beast depending on how many usage statistics are configured to be tracked. It is very active and write heavy. Since only one Usage and Health service application is allowed per farm, the database must be scaled up. If not attended to, this database could grow up to 1TB. Reduce retention time as well as what statistics are gathered for usage analytic purposes to keep this database at a maintainable size.

Subscription Settings Database

The Subscription Settings database is created when the Subscription Service Application is generated. This service application (and thus database) must be created from PowerShell commands and is used in conjunction with SharePoint Apps. This database should remain fairly small.

User Profile Service Databases

The User Profile Service Application uses several databases to carry out specific operations. They all default to a Simple recovery mode.

User Profile Database

This is the main database for the User Profile Service. The size and growth depends on the amount of SharePoint users on the farm as well as the usage of the newsfeed feature which includes tracking of user activities. This database can easily grow past 100GB.

User Profile Sync Database

The User Profile Sync database is used for the synchronization between the user profiles in SharePoint and the enterprise user source (typically Active Directory). This database can also get very large depending on the amount of users and groups within your enterprise structure.

User Profile Social Database

The User Profile Social database is used to store and maintain social tagging, ratings, and notes within the SharePoint farm. The size of this database can range from very small to very large depending on how much tagging, rating, and notes are entered across the SharePoint farm.

Word Automation Database

The Word Automation database is used for the Word Automation Service Application. This guy is not a threat and should stay fairly small. It defaults to a Full recovery model.

CHAPTER 2

Creating SharePoint Databases without GUIDs

This chapter explains how to create all of the SharePoint databases without the use of GUIDs in the name.

Overview

Overall, the rule-of-thumb when installing, configuring, and standing up SharePoint, is to take control and create everything manually, preferably using the command-line and PowerShell.

Running the SharePoint Products Configuration wizard after installation will create the Central Admin Content database with a GUID in the name. Running the Farm Configuration Wizard after creating the root web application and site collection will create all of the Service Applications selected using a GUID in the name of the database.

The answer? Don't run the wizards! The next sections explain how to avoid GUIDs in the database names.

Creating the Central Administration Content Database without a GUID

In order to avoid creating the Central Admin content database without a GUID, after the installation of SharePoint 2013, do not run the SharePoint Products Configuration wizard (make the check box is unchecked).

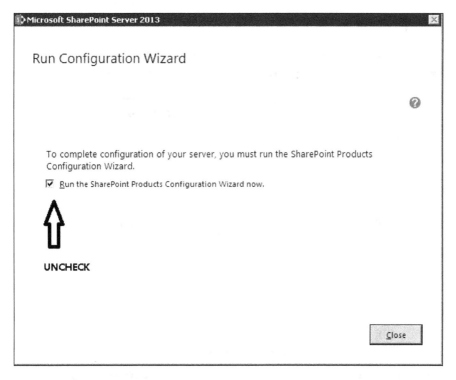

The SharePoint Products Configuration wizard is technically known as "PSCONFIG" (said as P S Config). The graphical wizard is launched from running a program file named *psconfigui.exe*, however, there is a command-line non-graphical version named PSCONFIG.exe. These programs are located under the BIN folder within the 15 hive (C:\Program Files\Common Files\Microsoft Shared\Web Server Extensions\15\BIN).

```
 Directory of C:\Program Files\Common Files\Microsoft Shared\Web Server Extensio
ns\15\BIN

10/01/2012   08:56 PM           549,032 PSCONFIG.EXE
10/01/2012   08:56 PM               273 PSCONFIG.EXE.CONFIG
10/01/2012   08:56 PM           799,424 psconfigui.exe
10/01/2012   08:56 PM               273 psconfigui.exe.config
              4 File(s)        1,349,002 bytes
              0 Dir(s)    41,236,733,952 bytes free

C:\Program Files\Common Files\Microsoft Shared\Web Server Extensions\15\BIN>_
```

In order to create the Central Admin database without a GUID,
you need to use the command-line version (PSCONFIG.EXE) of
PSCONFIG. You use it to create both the configuration database as
well as the admin content database. Here is the command syntax
for achieving this:

> psconfig -cmd configdb -create
> -server <<SQL Server Instance>>
> -database <<Configuration Database Name>>
> -admincontentdatabase <<Central Admin Content DB Name>>
> -user <<service account or farm admin>>
> -password <<password for account>>
> -passphrase <<new farm pass phrase>>

Unless the BIN folder location is part of the computer's PATH
property, you'll need to run this from the command-line at the BIN
location. The command and settings shown need to appear all on
one line.

Creating Service Application Databases without a GUID

The key here is to create each service application separately and not run through the farm configuration wizard within Central Admin. You may create each service application from the Central Admin UI or from scripted PowerShell.

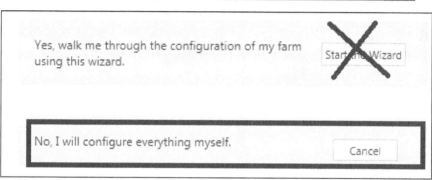

Creating Service Applications with PowerShell

It is recommended to create each service application using PowerShell. You can easily search the web and find plenty of examples for each service application. The key here is that you specify the database name within the cmdlet execution. Therefore, unless you have some kind of I-need-to-type-a-GUID-at-the-end-of-everything condition, there is no way the database will be created with a GUID.

Creating Service Applications from Central Admin

You may also create the service application databases without GUIDs from the Central Admin UI. All you need to do is modify the default database name within the dialogs:

```
Database Server
  SQLSP2013
Database Name
  lication_09af8a089cdc40cdbe7aa28d81ba783d
```

Not all dialogs allow you to change the database name. For the Search Service Application you will need to user PowerShell to insure GUIDs are not used. Although you can make sure GUIDs don't appear in most database names from the UI, using PowerShell provides you more control over how the databases are named.

CHAPTER 3

Understanding SQL Server Best Practices for Share-Point

This chapter discusses the recommended procedures and settings for managing SQL Server for SharePoint.

Dedicated Server

It is important to insure that SQL Server is running on a dedicated server for the SharePoint farm only. That is, no other non-SharePoint databases (or non-SQL Server system databases) are being run on the same server. Having additional transactions and I/O for external applications on the SQL Server would decrease SharePoint performance greatly. SharePoint needs its own server and instance.

SQL Server Settings

The following are recommended and required settings of SQL Server that should be applied *prior* to installing SharePoint.

Auto-Create Statistics

Do not enable auto-create statistics. This is not supported by SharePoint. SharePoint controls this setting during database provisioning.

DNS Aliases

It is recommended to create DNS aliases that point to the SQL Server IP Addresses for the SharePoint database instance such that maintenance is simplified.

Max Degree of Parallelism

The maximum degree of parallelism setting in SQL Server must be set to one (1) for SharePoint. The SharePoint installation won't continue anyway but to save the hassle, make sure it is set to 1 prior to installing. This insures that only one SQL Server processes tends to a request. My DBAs were a bit confused with this request and never heard of this requirement before - but that's what SharePoint wants and needs.

Security Hardening

Similar to the SQL Server Settings in the previous section, security hardening should occur **prior** to installing SharePoint. For SQL Server, security hardening for SharePoint involves the blocking of ports and the configuring of client aliases.

The default communication port for SQL Server is TCP Port 1433. SQL Server communicates instance information using UDP Port 1434. To fully secure SQL Server in a SharePoint farm, it is recommended to block both TCP Port 1433 and UDP Port 1434.

If you decide to block UDP Port 1434, you would then need to configure named instances of SQL Server to listen on a different port number. If you also block TCP Port 1433 then you have to assign a new port number to the default instance of SQL Server.

After you block these ports, all SharePoint servers in the farm need to have SQL Server client aliases configured such that they may communicate to SQL Server using the non-standard port assignments.

Unfortunately, in order to create SQL Server client aliases on your SharePoint servers, you must run SQL Server setup and install both the Connectivity Components and Management Tools. Once installed, a new alias is created by using the SQL Server Native Client Configuration from the SQL Server Configuration Manager.

Storage Optimization

Storage optimization pertains to the location of the SharePoint databases across physical disks. Overall, the tempdb database, content databases, usage database, search databases, and transaction logs should be placed on separate physical hard disks.

tempdb

If this is not entirely possible to separate all database types across separate physical disks, it is imperative that tempdb data files is stored on a drive that has dedicated disks allocated. It is also recommended to use a RAID 10 array for this drive.

The rule of thumb of tempdb is that each data file should be set to the same size and the number of data files should equal the amount of CPU cores on the server. This is a SQL Server optimization requirement not necessarily related to SharePoint. However, lack of following these guidelines would result in deprived SharePoint optimization.

Database and Transaction Logs

A similar SQL Server guideline which helps improve performance and mitigates data corruption, is to place the data files and transaction log files on separate disks.

Drive Speed Selection

Hopefully all of your drives are the same speed but we all know that as we get faster ones, the slower drives still stick around because of the need for space.

When selecting disk/drives for the various SQL databases involved in a SharePoint farm, make sure tempdb is running on the fastest. Next, for content databases containing sites that involve many updates, if you have to choose between disk speeds, favor the content database transaction logs on a faster drive and the content database data files on a slower one.

Conversely, for content databases that contain sites that are used primarily for read operations, favor the data files on the faster drive and the transaction logs on a slower one.

Content Database Data Files

For content databases that are heavily used, it is recommended to utilize multiple data files and if possible have them on their own disks. This may not be relevant for smaller content databases. I personally like smaller content databases (40-50GB) but it is recommended to keep them below 200GB in size. As you will see in the next chapter, it is easy to add additional content databases and take one or more offline to manage the size. It is recommended to prevent growth in this manner than to restrict the size of the database itself.

Specific Database Recommendations

Configuration database

The default recovery model for the configuration database is Full. It is recommended to change this to Simple in order to restrict the growth of the log file. Simple recovery mode is also essential if you are using database mirroring.

The other specific recommendation for the configuration database is to insure that the backup of the transaction log runs fairly regularly to force log truncation - keeping the database nice and tidy.

Central Administration Content Database

The Central Administration Content Database is included in the backup when a SharePoint farm configuration and content backup operation is performed. However, when the farm is restored, the Central Administration Content Database is not.

This is because the farm is online. Therefore, you should take the SharePoint farm offline first and then use SQL Server to backup and restore the Central Administration Content Database.

Search Databases

The Search Analytics database should be scaled out using a split operation. It only recommended to scale out this database if it begins to exceed 200GB. Personally I would probably start thinking about this when it reached 100-150GB.

It is recommended to scale out the Search Crawl database once you reach 20 million search items. This is performed by creating a new search crawl database.

The Search Link database should be placed on separate drive/disk/spindle if there are sites with very heavy traffic on your farm. The Search Link database should be scaled out by creating additional databases for every 60 million documents in the search crawl as well as for each 100 million queries you expect to encounter in each year.

Usage and Health Data Collection Database

Since the Usage and Health Data Collection database is very active, it should be put on a separate drive/disk/spindle. The only way to scale this database is up since there can only be one Usage and Health Data Collection Service Application on a SharePoint farm.

This page intentionally blank

CHAPTER 4

Working with

Content Databases

This chapter explores the management of content databases.

Adding New Content Database

Central Administration

To add a new content database via Central Administration, first click on Application Management from the left-hand navigation:

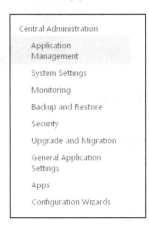

On the Application Management page, click on Manage content databases under the Databases section:

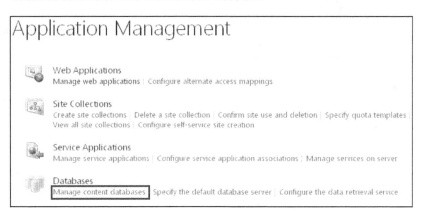

On the upper right-hand side of the screen, select the web application in which you want to add content databases:

Once selected, click on the Add Content Database link at the top left of the page:

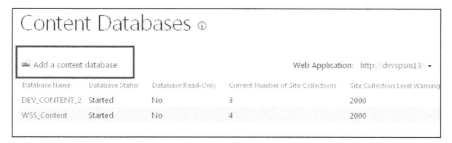

Enter the new database name and click OK:

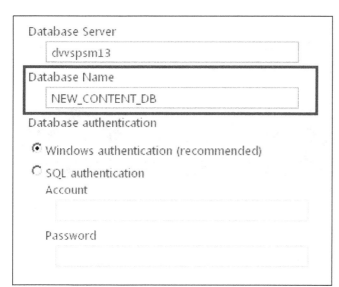

The database begins creation:

It may actually take a minute or two to provision.

When completed, the new content database appears in the list:

Database Name	Database Status	Database Read-Only	Current Number of Site Collections
DEV_CONTENT_2	Started	No	3
NEW_CONTENT_DB	Started	No	0
NEW_CONTENT_DB_PS	Started	No	0
WSS_Content	Started	No	4

PowerShell

It is very easy to create a new content database using PowerShell. First get a list of your web applications using Get-SPWebApplication:

Next, the cmdlet to create a new database is as follows:

New-SPContentDatabase -Name <<name of database>> -WebApplication <<name of web application>>

You may also provide the URL of the web application to the
-WebApplication parameter instead of the name.

```
PS F:\> New-SPContentDatabase -Name NEW_CONTENT_DB_PS -WebApplication "SharePoin
t - 80"

Id                : 59611046-03a3-4e17-b1aa-21e1c4ef4f5c
Name              : NEW_CONTENT_DB_PS
WebApplication    : SPWebApplication Name=SharePoint - 80
Server            : dvvspsm13
CurrentSiteCount  : 0
```

It may take a minute after you enter the statement but once
finished the information about the content database is displayed.

The new content database also appears in the list within Central
Admin:

Database Name	Database Status	Database Read-Only	Current Number of Site Collections
DEV_CONTENT_2	Started	No	3
NEW_CONTENT_DB	Started	No	0
NEW_CONTENT_DB_PS	Started	No	0
WSS_Content	Started	No	4

Removing a Content Database

Central Administration

To remove a content database, click on the content database from the Content Databases screen in Central Administration:

Database Name	Database Status	Database Read-Only
DEV_CONTENT_2	Started	No
NEW_CONTENT_DB	Started	No
NEW_CONTENT_DB_PS	Started	No
WSS_Content	Started	No

The Manage Content Database Settings page appears:

Manage Content Database Settings ⓘ

Warning: this page is not encrypted for secure communication. User names, passwords, and any other i

Database Information

Specify database connection settings for this content database. Use the **Database status** options to control whether or not new Site Collections can be created in the database. When the database status is set to **Ready**, the database is available for hosting new Site Collections. When the database status is set to **Offline**, no new Site Collections can be created.

Database server
dvvspsm13

SQL Server database name
NEW_CONTENT_DB_PS

Database status
Ready ▼

Database Read-Only
No

Database authentication
Windows authentication

Scroll down the page and find the Remove Content Database section:

Remove Content Database

Use this section to remove a content database from the server farm.
When you select the **Remove content database** check box and click
OK, the database is no longer associated with this Web application.
Caution: When you remove the content database, any sites listed in
that content database are removed from the server farm, but the site
data remains in the database.

☐ Remove content database

Simply check the Remove content database checkbox and click OK:

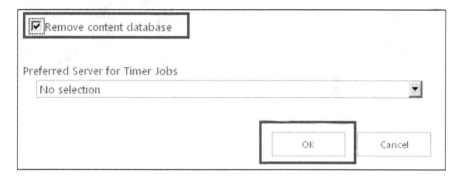

The content database is removed from the web application:

Database Name	Database Status	Database Read-Only	Current Number of Site Collections
DEV_CONTENT_2	Started	No	3
NEW_CONTENT_DB	Started	No	0
WSS_Content	Started	No	4

NOTE: WHEN YOU REMOVE A CONTENT DATABASE, THE DATABASE STILL EXISTS IN SQL SERVER

PowerShell

To remove a content database from SharePoint using PowerShell, use the Dismount-SPContentDatabase and provide the name of the database as follows:

Dismount-SPContentDatabase -Identity <<name of database>>

```
Administrator: SharePoint 2013 Management Shell                          _ □ X
PS F:\> Dismount-SPContentDatabase -Identity "NEW_CONTENT_DB"

Confirm
Are you sure you want to perform this action?
Performing operation "Dismount-SPContentDatabase" on Target "NEW_CONTENT_DB".
[Y] Yes  [A] Yes to All  [N] No  [L] No to All  [S] Suspend  [?] Help
<default is "Y">:y
PS F:\> _
```

Enter 'y' to confirm the operation.

The content database is removed from SharePoint:

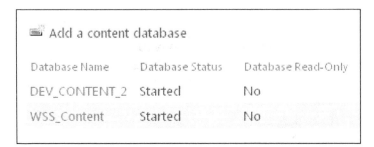

Database Name	Database Status	Database Read-Only
DEV_CONTENT_2	Started	No
WSS_Content	Started	No

THIS DOES NOT REMOVE THE DATABASE FROM SQL SERVER

To remove a content database from SharePoint and SQL Server altogether, use the Remove-SPContentDatabase cmdlet as follows:

Remove-SPContentDatabase -Identity <<name of database>>

```
Administrator: SharePoint 2013 Management Shell
PS F:\> Remove-SPContentDatabase -Identity "NEW_CONTENT_DB"

Confirm
Are you sure you want to perform this action?
Performing operation "Remove-SPContentDatabase" on Target "NEW_CONTENT_DB".
[Y] Yes  [A] Yes to All  [N] No  [L] No to All  [S] Suspend  [?] Help
(default is "Y"):y

Confirm
Removing 'NEW_CONTENT_DB' will permananetly delete the SQL database,
permananetly deleting all content stored within it. Use
Dismount-SPContentDatabase if you do not want to delete the SQL database.
[Y] Yes  [A] Yes to All  [N] No  [L] No to All  [S] Suspend  [?] Help
(default is "Y"):y
PS F:\>
```

You will be prompted for the Remove operation and then again for deleting the database from SQL Server.

The database is removed from SharePoint and SQL Server now.

Attaching an Existing Content Database

A common scenario here is the backup and restore of a content database from one SharePoint farm to another (e.g. from Production to Stage). Nonetheless, the content database exists on the SQL Server but SharePoint knows nothing about it at the moment.

Central Administration

To attach a content database from Central Administration, first click on Application Management from the left-hand navigation:

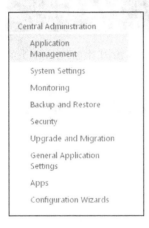

On the Application Management page, click on Manage content databases under the Databases section:

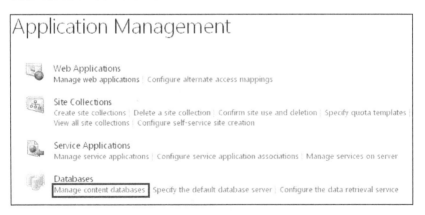

On the upper right-hand side of the screen, select the web application in which you want to add content databases:

Once selected, click on the Add Content Database link at the top left of the page:

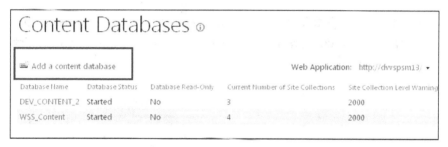

NOW HERE IS THE TRICK!!

It is not obvious since this page is used to create a brand new content database, however, if you enter a name of a content database that already exists in SQL Server, the content database will be attached (instead of being created).

Database Server

dvvspsm13

Database Name

ATTACH_CONTENT_DB|

Click OK.

This time it won't take too long since a database doesn't need to be created. The content database is attached and added to the list of databases for the selected web application:

Database Name	Database Status	Database Read-Only
ATTACH_CONTENT_DB	Started	No
DEV_CONTENT_2	Started	No
WSS_Content	Started	No

PowerShell

To attach a content database from PowerShell, use the Mount-SPContentDatabase as follows:

Mount-SPContentDatabase -Name <<name of database>> -WebApplication <<name or URL of web application>>

```
PS F:\> Mount-SPContentDatabase -Name "ATTACH_CONTENT_DB" -WebApplication "Share
Point - 80"

Id                : ff93a27c-8ad0-40bb-974f-5ed94d2a8094
Name              : ATTACH_CONTENT_DB
WebApplication    : SPWebApplication Name=SharePoint - 80
Server            : dvvspsm13
CurrentSiteCount  : 0
```

You may list out the content databases using Get-SPContentDatabase:

```
PS F:\> Get-SPContentDatabase

Id                : d2092c8b-6237-4042-a261-70bed209439d
Name              : WSS_Content_20222
WebApplication    : SPWebApplication Name=SharePoint - 20222
Server            : dvvspsm13
CurrentSiteCount  : 2

Id                : afe052dd-3f7f-494d-9aa6-d9487235538a
Name              : WSS_Content
WebApplication    : SPWebApplication Name=SharePoint - 80
Server            : dvvspsm13
CurrentSiteCount  : 4

Id                : eb64b2d7-1ae5-47ed-89a6-a3e1dd521128
Name              : DEV_CONTENT_2
WebApplication    : SPWebApplication Name=SharePoint - 80
Server            : dvvspsm13
CurrentSiteCount  : 3

Id                : ff93a27c-8ad0-40bb-974f-5ed94d2a8094
Name              : ATTACH_CONTENT_DB
WebApplication    : SPWebApplication Name=SharePoint - 80
Server            : dvvspsm13
CurrentSiteCount  : 0
```

Capping a Content Database

When one of your content databases contains a large amount of site collections and/or becomes large in size, you may not want that particular content database to get any larger. Therefore you can easily "cap" the content database by taking it offline. This sounds like it is not available for use but it just means that that content database won't be used to create any new site collections.

Central Administration

To stop a content database via Central Administration, first click on Application Management from the left-hand navigation:

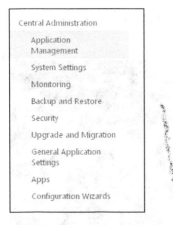

On the Application Management page, click on Manage content databases under the Databases section:

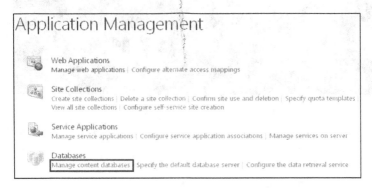

On the upper right-hand side of the screen, select the web application in which you want to add content databases:

Once selected, click on the content database you wish to "cap" from the list:

Database Name	Database Status	Database Read-Only
ATTACH_CONTENT_DB	Started	No
DEV_CONTENT_2	Started	No
WSS_Content	Started	No

The Manage Content Database Settings page appears.

Right at the top section locate the Database status and use the drop-down to change from Ready to Offline:

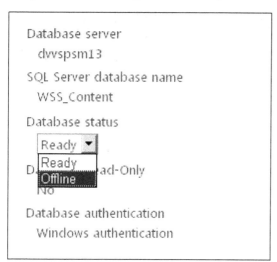

Scroll down and click OK.

The content database is now "Stopped":

Database Name	Database Status	Database Read-Only
ATTACH_CONTENT_DB	Started	No
DEV_CONTENT_2	Started	No
WSS_Content	Stopped	No

You don't have to worry about new sites being created within the stopped content database. However the size may still grow by more content being uploaded to the existing site collections in the database.

PowerShell

To take a content database offline using PowerShell, simply use the Set-SPContentDatabase cmdlet as follows:

Set-SPContentDatabase -Identity <<name of database>> -Status 1

There is no response, however, Get-SPContentDatabase won't display content databases that are Offline.

To turn a content database back to Ready, use **-Status 0**.

Controlling Which Content Database is Used for Site Collection Creation

Now that you have seen how to take content databases offline such that they won't be used for new site collection creation, it is only a matter of logic to figure out how to force new site collections to be created within a specific content database.

To force new site collections to be created within a single content database, simply take all of the content databases Offline except for the one in which you want the site collections to be created.

Listing the Site Collections Contained within a Content Database

Before you move site collections around content databases, it would be nice to know which site collections exist in each content database as well as the size. This can be easily facilitated using PowerShell.

Getting the Site Collections of a Content Database

To list out the site collections use Get-SPSite with the -ContentDatabase parameter as follows:

Get-SPSite -ContentDatabase <<name of content database>>

```
Administrator: SharePoint 2013 Management Shell
PS F:\> Get-SPSite -ContentDatabase WSS_CONTENT

Url
---
http://dvvspsm13
http://dvvspsm13/sites/Apps
http://dvvspsm13/sites/dev
http://dvvspsm13/sites/SearchCenter


PS F:\> _
```

Retrieving the Sizes of Site Collections within a Content Database

It is nice to see what site collections are in a particular content database but what about the size? Knowing the size may help in trying to balance out your content databases.

Therefore, I modified a PowerShell cmdlet line from Todd Klindt to retrieve the sizes of the site collections within a particular content database. The cmdlet line is as follows:

Get-SPSite -ContentDatabase <<name of content database>>| select url, @{label="Size in MB";Expression={$_.usage.storage/1MB}} | Sort-Object -Descending -Property "Size in MB"

```
PS F:\> Get-SPSite -ContentDatabase WSS_CONTENT | select url, @{label="Size in M
B";Expression={$_.usage.storage/1MB}} | Sort-Object -Descending -Property "Size
in MB"

Url                                                                   Size in MB
---                                                                   ----------
http://dvvspsm13                                                 18.5088090896606
http://dvvspsm13/sites/Apps                                      6.34929275512695
http://dvvspsm13/sites/SearchCenter                              3.91324710845947
http://dvvspsm13/sites/dev                                       1.99415302276611
```

Adapted with permission from:
http://www.toddklindt.com/blog/Lists/Posts/Post.aspx?ID=270

Moving a Site Collection to a Different Content Database

Now that there is an easy way to see what site collections exist in each content database as well as the sizes, you may want to move things around to balance out the storage usage.

You can run the PowerShell commands explained in the previous section against different content databases to see what you may want to move:

```
PS F:\> Get-SPSite -ContentDatabase WSS_CONTENT | select url, @{label="Size in M
B";Expression={$_.usage.storage/1MB}} | Sort-Object -Descending -Property "Size
in MB"

Url                                                   Size in MB
---                                                   ----------
http://dvvspsm13                                      18.5088090896606
http://dvvspsm13/sites/Apps                           6.34929275512695
http://dvvspsm13/sites/SearchCenter                   3.91324710845947
http://dvvspsm13/sites/dev                            1.99415302276611

PS F:\> Get-SPSite -ContentDatabase DEV_CONTENT_2 | select url, @{label="Size in
 MB";Expression={$_.usage.storage/1MB}} | Sort-Object -Descending -Property "Siz
e in MB"

Url                                                   Size in MB
---                                                   ----------
http://dvvspsm13/sites/DevSite                        3.01433944702148
http://dvvspsm13/sites/AppBlog                        1.90998458862305
http://dvvspsm13/sites/MySites                        1.42262840270996
```

In my example WSS_CONTENT contains the bulk of content in regards to storage space. DEV_CONTENT_2 is relatively small. Based on the output of the sizes, I may want to move my Apps site collection from WSS_CONTENT to DEV_CONTENT2.

To move site collections between content databases, use the Move-SPSite cmdlet as follows:

Move-SPSite -Identity <<url of site collection >> -DestinationDatabase <<name of content database>>

```
PS F:\> Move-SPSIte -Identity http://dvvspsm13/sites/apps  -DestinationDatabase
DEV_CONTENT_2

Confirm
Are you sure you want to perform this action?
Performing operation "Move-SPSite" on Target "http://dvvspsm13/sites/apps".
[Y] Yes  [A] Yes to All  [N] No  [L] No to All  [S] Suspend  [?] Help
(default is "Y"):y
WARNING: IIS must be restarted before this change will take effect. To restart
IIS, open a command prompt window and type iisreset.
PS F:\> _
```

You will be prompted to perform the action. Enter 'y' to confirm
the move of the site collection. After the operation has been
completed, you need to reset IIS (using IISReset):

```
PS F:\> iisreset

Attempting stop...
Internet services successfully stopped
Attempting start...
Internet services successfully restarted
PS F:\> _
```

Retrieving the sites from the content database again shows that
the Apps site collection is now in DEV_CONTENT_DB:

```
PS F:\> Get-SPSite -ContentDatabase DEV_CONTENT_2

Url
---
http://dvvspsm13/sites/AppBlog
http://dvvspsm13/sites/DevSite
http://dvvspsm13/sites/MySites


PS F:\> _
```

What? It's not there.

Looking in Central Admin under View Site Collections shows that the Apps site collection is indeed in DEV_CONTENT_2:

URL		URL	http://dvvspsm13/sites/Apps
/		Title	Apps
/sites/AppBlog		Description	
/sites/Apps		Primary administrator:	Mann, Steven
/sites/dev		E-mail address:	smann@morganlewis.com
/sites/DevSite		Database Name	DEV_CONTENT_2
/sites/MySites			

Like many things in SharePoint, objects and collections become cached on the server or within sessions. That is what is happening in this case. If you open a new SharePoint PowerShell window and issue the command, you'll see that the site collection has indeed been moved and appears in the list:

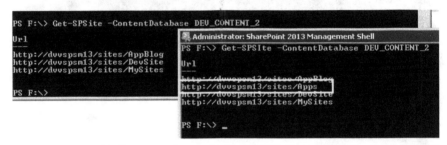

However you don't need to do that. Issuing Get-SPSite by itself will reload all of the sites such that when using the -ContentDatabase parameter afterwards results in the correct list.

```
PS F:\> Get-SPSite

Url
---
http://dvvspsm13:20222
http://dvvspsm13:20222/personal/mp
http://dvvspsm13
http://dvvspsm13/sites/AppBlog
http://dvvspsm13/sites/Apps
http://dvvspsm13/sites/dev
http://dvvspsm13/sites/DevSite
http://dvvspsm13/sites/MySites
http://dvvspsm13/sites/SearchCenter

PS F:\> Get-SPSite -ContentDatabase DEV_CONTENT_2

Url
---
http://dvvspsm13/sites/AppBlog
http://dvvspsm13/sites/Apps
http://dvvspsm13/sites/DevSite
http://dvvspsm13/sites/MySites

PS F:\> _
```

CHAPTER 5

Backing Up SharePoint 2013 Components

Backing Up the Farm

Central Administration

To back up the farm using Central Administration, from the main screen under the Backup and Restore section click on the Performa backup link:

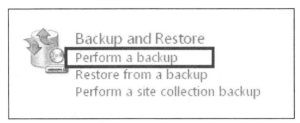

The Perform a Backup page appears:

Check the Farm checkbox:

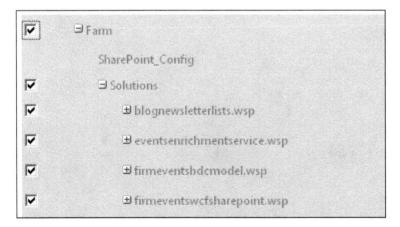

The rest of of the checkboxes are selected and the entire section turns blue.

Scroll down to the bottom of the page and click Next:

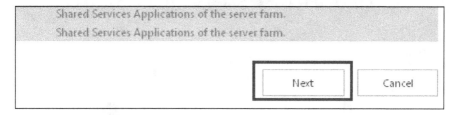

The backup option page appears:

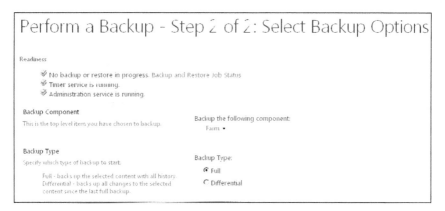

Enter the backup location in the Backup location text box and click the Start Backup button:

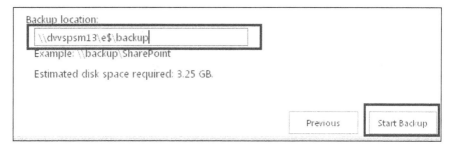

The Backup and Restore Job Status page appears.

Backup and Restore Job Status ⓘ

Readiness

> ⚲ A backup or restore is currently in progress.

⚪ Timer service is running.

⚪ Administration service is running.

Preparing current backup/restore job. If the backup/restore job does not begin after five minutes,

🖹 Refresh | 🔍 View History

There are no current or recent backup or restore processes to show. If you recently started a backu
appear.

The page will auto-refresh and display the status of all farm items:

Phase	In process
Item (Current/Total)	42/203 (Farm\Microsoft SharePoint Foundation Web Application\SharePoint - 20222\job-workflow-failover)
Start Time	12/15/2013 6:16 PM
Top Component	Farm
Backup ID	7dd4fc5d-2da9-476f-ae88-03b2ab189279
Directory	\\dvvspsm13\e$\backup\spbr0009\
Backup Method	Full
Backup Threads	3
Warnings	6
Errors	0

Name	Progress	Last Update
Farm	In process	12/15/2013 6:16 PM
SharePoint_Config	In process	12/15/2013 6:16 PM
Solutions	In process	12/15/2013 6:16 PM

It may take several minutes to complete depending on the size of your farm.

PowerShell

To backup the farm using PowerShell, execute the Backup-SPFarm cmdlet as follows:

Backup-SPFarm -Directory <<BackupPath>> -BackupMethod {Full | Differential}

```
Administrator: SharePoint 2013 Management Shell
PS F:\> Backup-SPFarm -Directory \\dvvspsm13\e$\backup -BackupMethod FULL
```

The farm components are backed up to the folder specified.

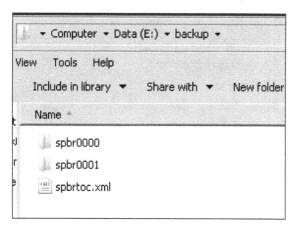

Backing Up a Content Database

Central Administration

To back up a content database using Central Administration, from the main screen under the Backup and Restore section click on the Performa backup link:

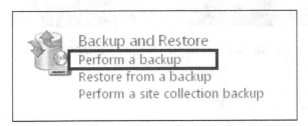

The Perform a Backup page appears:

Check the content database to backup:

☐	⊟ SharePoint - 80	Web Application
☐	WSS_Content	Content Database
☑	DEV_CONTENT_2	Content Database
☐	ATTACH_CONTENT_DB	Content Database

Scroll down to the bottom of the page and click Next:

The backup option page appears:

Perform a Backup - Step 2 of 2: Select Backup Options ⊙

Readiness

 ✓ No backup or restore in progress. Backup and Restore Job Status
 ✓ Timer service is running.
 ✓ Administration service is running.

Backup Component
This is the top level item you have chosen to backup.

Backup the following component:
Farm\Microsoft SharePoint Foundation Web Application\SharePoint - 80\DEV_CONTENT_2 ▾

Enter the backup location in the Backup location text box and click the Start Backup button:

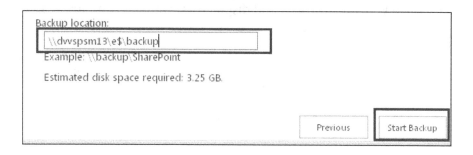

The Backup and Restore Job Status page appears.

Backup and Restore Job Status ⓘ

Readiness

> ⚙ A backup or restore is currently in progress.

⚙ Timer service is running.

⚙ Administration service is running.

Preparing current backup/restore job. If the backup/restore job does not begin after five minutes,

📄 Refresh | 🔍 View History

There are no current or recent backup or restore processes to show. If you recently started a backu
appear.

The page will auto-refresh and display the status of the backup:

Phase	In process
Item (Current/Total)	1/1 (Farm\Microsoft SharePoint Foundation Web Application\SharePoint - 80\DEV_CONTENT_2)
Start Time	12/15/2013 6:57 PM
Top Component	Farm\Microsoft SharePoint Foundation Web Application\SharePoint - 80\DEV_CONTENT_2
Backup ID	a082bb28-b632-4044-8b1f-b76447bf43e8
Directory	\\dvvspsm13\e$\backup\spbr0002\
Backup Method	Full
Backup Threads	3
Warnings	0
Errors	0

It may take several minutes to complete depending on the size of your content database.

PowerShell

To backup a content database using PowerShell, execute the Backup-SPFarm cmdlet with the -Item parameter as follows:

Backup-SPFarm -Directory <<BackupPath>> -BackupMethod {Full | Differential}

      -Item <<ContentDatabaseName>>

```
PS F:\> Backup-SPFarm -Directory \\dvvspsm13\e$\backup -BackupMethod FULL
        -Item DEV_CONTENT_2
```

The content database is backed up to the folder specified.

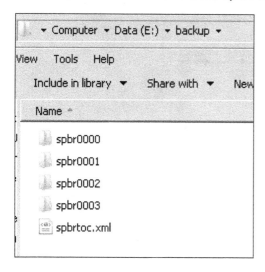

Backing Up a Site Collection

Central Administration

To back up a site collection using Central Administration, from the main screen under the Backup and Restore section click on the Performa backup link:

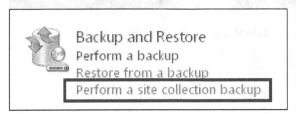

The Site Collection Backup page appears:

Select Change Site Collection from the Site Collection drop-down menu:

The Select Site Collection dialog appears:

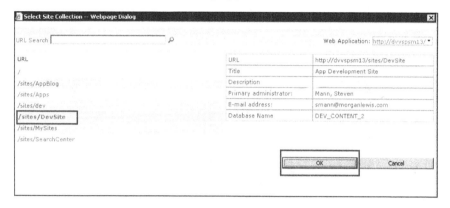

Select the site collection to backup and click OK.

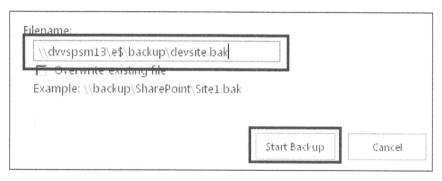

Enter the file location and **name** in the Filename text box and click Start Backup.

The Granular Backup Job Status page appears:

Granular Backup Job Status ⓘ

Readiness

A site collection backup is currently in progress.

No export is in progress.

Timer service is running.

🖹 Refresh | ✖ Delete Backup Job

Site Collection Backup

The page will auto-refresh and display the status of the backup:

Site Collection Backup

Current Job

Status	No operation in progress.

Previous Job

Status	Succeeded
Completed	12/15/2013 7:15 PM
Duration (hh:mm:ss)	0:00:19
Recovery Step	To recover the data, use the PowerShell restore command Restore-SPSite. For more details, type Restore-SPSite -? at the PowerShell command prompt.

Content Export

Current Job

Status	No operation in progress.

Previous Job

Status	No previous job.

It may take several minutes to complete depending on the size of your content database.

PowerShell

To backup a content database using PowerShell, execute the Backup-SPSite cmdlet with the -Item parameter as follows:

Backup-SPSite -Identity <<URL of Site Collection>> -Path <<Backup Path and File-name>>

```
PS F:\> Backup-SPSite -Identity http://dvvspsm13/sites/DevSite -Path \\dvvspsm13
\e$\backup\devsite_backup_from_PS.bak
PS F:\> _
```

The site collection is backed up to the backup file specified:

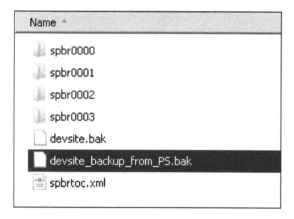

THIS PAGE INTENTIONALLY
BLANK

CHAPTER 6

Restoring SharePoint 2013 Components

Restoring a Farm Backup

Central Administration

To restore a farm backup using Central Administration, from the main screen under the Backup and Restore section click on the Restore from a backup link:

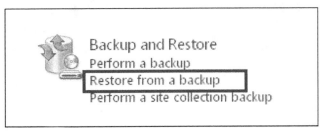

The Backup and Restore History page appears:

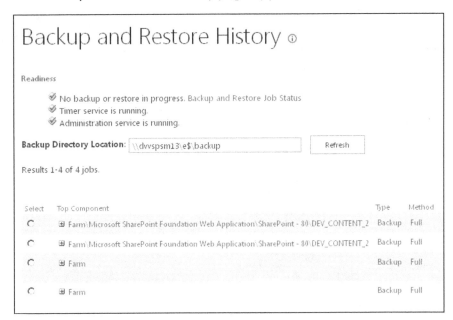

Select the Farm backup to restore and click Next:

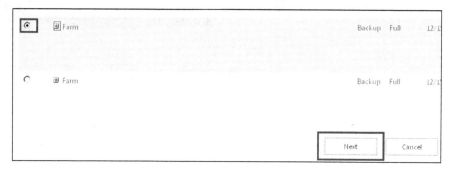

The Select Component to Restore page appears:

Select the Farm component:

The rest of of the checkboxes are selected and the entire section turns blue.

Scroll down to the bottom of the page and click Next:

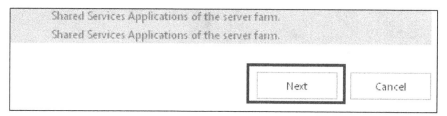

The Restore Options page appears:

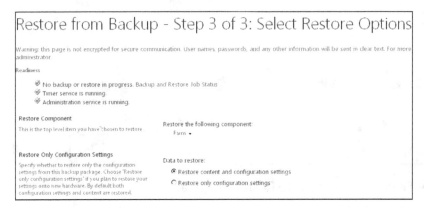

If you are restoring on top of the existing farm change the type to Same configuration:

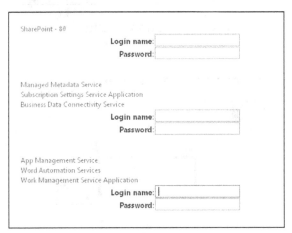

Next, enter the service account login and passwords for the web/service applications listed:

Scroll down and click on the Start Restore button:

The Backup and Restore Job Status page appears:

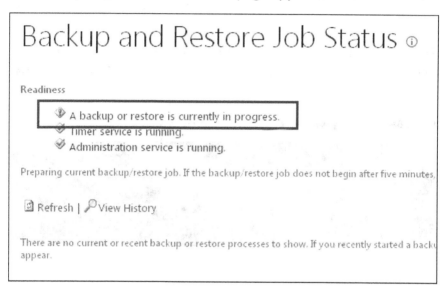

The page will auto-refresh and display the status of the restore. It may take several minutes to complete depending on the size of your farm.

PowerShell

To restore from a farm backup using PowerShell, execute the Restore-SPFarm cmdlet as follows:

Restore-SPFarm -Directory <<Backup Path>> -RestoreMethod Overwrite

-BackupId <<Backup GUID>>

The -BackupID parameter is optional and the latest farm backup will be restored if not specified. You may use Get-SPBackupHistory to obtain the backup GUID:

Get-SPBackupHistory -Directory <<Backup Path>> -ShowBackup

```
PS F:\> Get-SPBackupHistory -Directory \\dvvspsm13\e$\backup -ShowBackup

T S Operation ID                                 Method   Start Time
- - ------------                                 ------   ----------
B N 4c1e5858-c758-4899-9a76-715f07f05a5e         Full
B N a082bb28-b632-4044-8b1f-b76447bf43e8         Full
B N 54f5f462-9591-4e0b-83ea-59cccc7f0950         Full
B N 7dd4fc5d-2da9-476f-ae88-03b2ab189279         Full

PS F:\> _
```

Restoring a Content Database from a Backup

Central Administration

To restore a content database from a backup using Central Administration, from the main screen under the Backup and Restore section click on the Restore from a backup link:

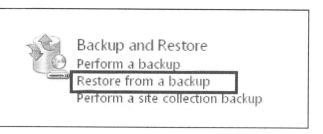

The Backup and Restore History page appears:

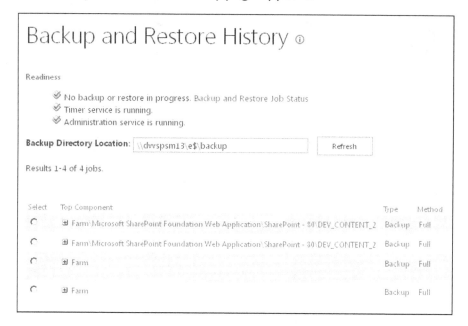

Select the Content Database backup to restore and click Next:

The Select Component to Restore page appears:

Select the Content Database component from the list:

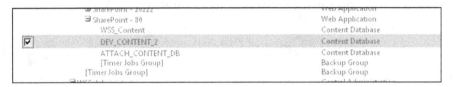

Scroll down to the bottom of the page and click Next:

The Restore Options page appears:

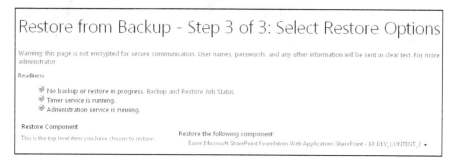

If you are restoring on top of the existing content database change the type to Same configuration:

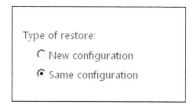

Scroll down and click on the Start Restore button:

The Backup and Restore Job Status page appears:

Backup and Restore Job Status ⓘ

Readiness

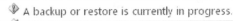 A backup or restore is currently in progress.

Timer service is running.

Administration service is running.

Preparing current backup/restore job. If the backup/restore job does not begin after five minutes,

🗐 Refresh | 🔎View History

There are no current or recent backup or restore processes to show. If you recently started a backu
appear.

The page will auto-refresh and display the status of the restore. It may take several minutes to complete depending on the size of your content database.

PowerShell

To restore a content database from a backup using PowerShell, execute the Restore-SPFarm cmdlet with the -Item parameter as follows:

Restore-SPFarm -Directory <<Backup Path>> -RestoreMethod Overwrite

-BackupId <<Backup GUID>> -Item <<Content Database Name>>

The -BackupID parameter is optional and the latest backup will be restored if not specified. You may use Get-SPBackupHistory to obtain the backup GUID:

Get-SPBackupHistory -Directory <<Backup Path>> -ShowBackup

```
PS F:\> Get-SPBackupHistory -Directory \\dvvspsm13\e$\backup -ShowBackup

T S Operation ID                            Method    Start Time
- - ------------                            ------    ----------
B N 4c1e5858-c758-4899-9a76-715f07f05a5e    Full
B N a082bb28-b632-4044-8b1f-b76447bf43e8    Full
B N 54f5f462-9591-4e0b-83ea-59cccc7f0950    Full
B N 7dd4fc5d-2da9-476f-ae88-03b2ab189279    Full

PS F:\> _
```

Restoring a Site Collection from a Backup File

The only way to restore a site collection from a backup file is through PowerShell. The restore is performed using the Restore-SPSite cmdlet as follows:

Restore-SPSite -Identity <<URL of Site Collection>> -Path <<Path and filename of backup>>

If the site collection already exists and you want to overwrite the existing site collection with the backup, include the -Force parameter.

```
PS F:\> Restore-SPSite -Identity http://dvvspsm13/sites/DevSite -Path \\dvvspsm1
3\e$\backup\devsite_backup_from_PS.bak -Force

Confirm
Are you sure you want to perform this action?
Performing operation "Restore-SPSite" on Target
"http://dvvspsm13/sites/DevSite".
[Y] Yes  [A] Yes to All  [N] No  [L] No to All  [S] Suspend  [?] Help
(default is "Y"):y
PS F:\>
```

CHAPTER 7

Understanding Best Practices for Backup and Recovery

Performance Recommendations

Backup Location

It is recommended to perform SQL Server backups to local drives first and then move them around to network drives for sharing/restore purposes. This allows the backup process to complete quicker and more efficiently.

It is also recommended for the local drive not to be one in which SQL Server is running (e.g. C:) and preferably not a drive that contains the data or log files. This avoids I/O contentions.

Eliminate Conflicts

To avoid processing conflicts and performance degradation, it is recommended to perform backups during times of less usage. Running incremental backups during business hours is more acceptable (and less noticeable). Space out the incremental backups across databases throughout the day such that there is no convergence of disk I/O, memory, and/or processor (CPU) usages.

Maintain Smaller Databases

Smaller databases mean smaller backup and recovery times. They are more manageable and the backup files are also. Many times we have had trouble trying to backup our three content databases because there was not enough room on the drive to store all three backups. We needed to do each one separately and then wait (what seemed hours) to copy the backup file to a different location.

As I have stated throughout this book, I'd rather have five 40GB content databases than one 200GB content database. It makes life so much easier when your databases are smaller.

Backup Compression

Using backup compression makes the backup files even more manageability and easily moveable around the network. Using backup compression also actually makes the backup run faster as the backup process does not have to write as much data to the backup file and the compression process occurs in memory.

RAID Usage

If you are using RAID on your backup device it is recommended to use RAID 10 and to avoid RAID 5. RAID 5 has slower write performance because of parity management. RAID 10 doesn't need to manage parity and is much faster.

Backing Up the Farm with PowerShell

When using the Backup-SPFarm in PowerShell, there is a -BackupThreads parameter that you may use to tweak the amount of threads. The default 3 and the maximum is 10. Increasing the amount of threads consumes more resources during the backup but decreases the overall duration. You may need to find the right balance here.

Backing Up Site Collections

If your site collection is under 15GB, it is recommended simply to use Backup-SPSite in PowerShell. It is quick and easy. Once your site collection grows past 15GB but still under 100GB, it is recommended to use the backup within Central Administration as the processing is performed asynchronously behind the scenes. In other words, you won't have a PowerShell command window lock up and become unresponsive: potentially corrupting the backup process.

Once your site collection is over 100GB (which I hope never happens), you are pretty much locked into backing up the entire content database from SQL Server. It is not recommended to perform the content database backup from Central Admin.

Procedural Recommendations

Deployment and Configuration Documentation

It is a good idea to document all of the managed accounts and configuration settings used in building out your SharePoint farm. This helps in the recovery process. As you have seen in some of the screens when restoring a farm, the managed accounts and passwords are needed for the service applications.

Remote Blob Storage Backups

If you have implemented Remote Blob Storage (RBS) using the FILESTREAM Provider (i.e. Out-of-the-box implementation as explained in the next chapter), both SQL Server and SharePoint include the RBS during backup and restore of content databases. However, other Microsoft and/or third-party backup/restore solutions may not support RBS via the FILESTREAM Provider.

Therefore it is recommended to only use SQL Server or SharePoint to backup and restore using RBS. If you are using a third-party solution to implement RBS, it is recommended to use that third-party's backup/restore process.

Recovery Environment

While this may not be economical, it is recommended to have a recovery environment ready to be able to restore SharePoint and keep your intranet, internet, and/or extranet up and running in case of a critical disaster.

Most of the time this only needs to be a backup database server as there should be redundant web front ends and application servers for load-balancing and fault tolerance anyway.

If you can't afford for SharePoint to be down then you need to afford backup hardware - at least for interim purposes.

Scheduled Backups

It is important to have backups on regular schedules preferably during times when there is little or no activity (e.g. overnight). You may use PowerShell and the Task Scheduler to automate backup scripts.

Server Names

When accessing servers across different domains, it is recommended to use fully qualified domain names (FQDN). This insures accessibility and avoids network/connection issues.

Quality Assurance Recommendations

Back up SharePoint Server Files

The files that live on your SharePoint servers are not all included in the backup processes.

This may include the following:

- Web directory files and web.config files
- Custom CSS and JS files
- DLLs in the bin folder or GAC
- Custom User Controls
- ULS Logs
- Any other customized SharePoint file not deployed as a solution

Personally I don't really care about ULS logs after they are a day old. I usually replicate any issues and then find the problems reported in the ULS logs. What happened yesterday, last week, or last month is no concern. Some may feel differently and want to keep the ULS logs around. That's fine – it is recommended.

Anyway, it is good to have backups of any customized files and configurations such that full recovery may be facilitated quickly and easily.

Disk Space for Backups

Always make sure you have enough disk space to perform backups – especially automatically scheduled backups where you may assume it is running successfully. Of course keeping the content databases small and using backup compression helps in the amount of free space required for a backup.

Off-Site Copies

Most companies today keep copies of backups off-site. It is always a good idea just in case there are physical disasters on-site.

Test Backup/Restore

It is a good idea to periodically test your backups by performing restores in other environments. This keeps the process fresh in your head and when issues occur, you'll be ready to resolve them instead of fumbling with the restore operations. This also keeps the backup integrity in check and validates your backup processes along with your recovery hardware.

CHAPTER 8

Implementing Remote Blob Storage in SharePoint 2013

This chapter outlines steps and configurations to implement Remote Blob Storage (RBS) in SharePoint 2013 using SQL Server 2012. The steps are similar for SQL Server 2008 R2.

One of the advantages with the latest SharePoint versions and SQL Server versions is the ability to implement RBS using the FileStream Provider. This allows for documents and files that are larger than a specified amount of bytes (default 100KB) to be stored on a connected file system of the SQL Server box instead of inside the database itself. The overall advantage is keeping your content databases smaller and more manageable.

Enable File Stream on the SQL Server

On the SQL Server 2012 box, open SQL Server Configurations Manager.

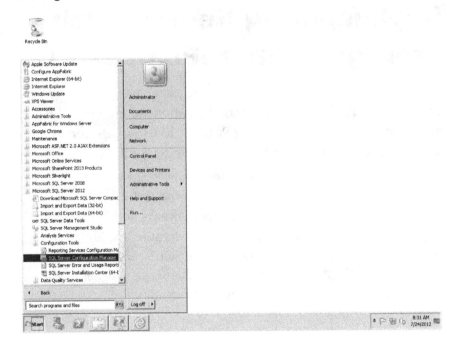

Select SQL Server Services from the left pane. Right-click on the SQL Server process in the right window and select Properties:

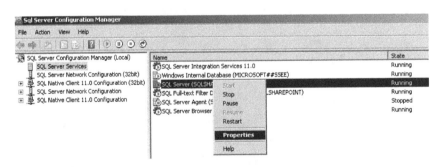

The SQL Server Properties dialog appears. Select the FILESTREAM tab and check all of the check boxes:

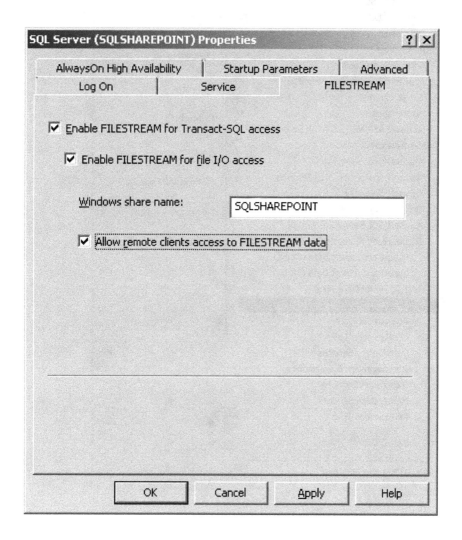

Click OK.

Start SQL Management Studio and open a new query window.

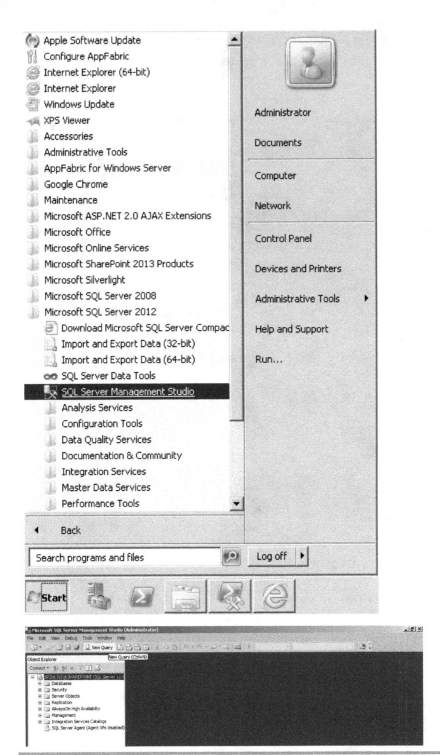

Execute the following two SQL Statements (on any database):

EXEC sp_configure filestream_access_level, 2

RECONFIGURE

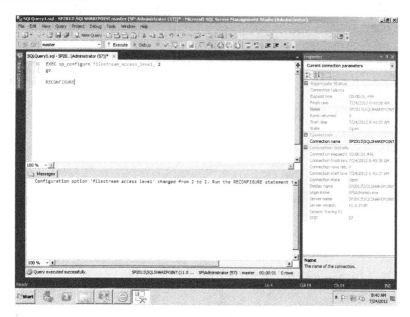

Using your content database open a new query:

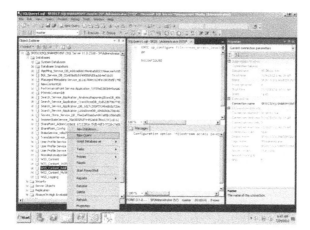

Create the master key using the following SQL:

if not exists (select * from sys.symmetric_keys where name = N'##MS_DatabaseMasterKey##')
    create master key encryption by password = N'Admin Key Password !2#4'

```
SQLQuery2.sql - SP20...\Administrator (65))*  ×
  use WSS_Content_6ddf1a64a957436589e0a80ad67f9301

  if not exists (select * from sys.symmetric_keys where name =
      N'##MS_DatabaseMasterKey##')create master key encryption by
      password = N'Admin Key Password !2#4'
```

It is very important that the password is !2#4 - RBS will not work properly if this is not the password used.

Create a new filegroup for the RBS:

if not exists (select groupname from sysfilegroups where group-name=N'RBSFilestreamProvider')
    alter database [<your content database>]
    add filegroup RBSFilestreamProvider contains filestream

```
SQLQuery3.sql - SP20...Administrator (131))*   SQLQuery2.sql - SP20...\Administrator (52))*  ×  SQLQuery1.sql - SP20...\Administrator (57))*
  if not exists (select groupname from sysfilegroups where groupname=N'RBSFilestreamProvider')
  alter database WSS_Content_6ddf1a64a957436589e0a80ad67f9301 add
      filegroup RBSFilestreamProvider contains filestream
```

100%

Add the "file" using the following SQL:

alter database [<your content database>]
add file (name = RBSFilestreamFile, filename= 'c:\SPBlobStorage')
  to filegroup RBSFilestreamProvider

The "file" is a folder on a connected drive. It can be a local drive
on the SQL Server or an attached iSCSI drive. The folder cannot
exist already. Executing the SQL statement above automatically
creates the folder specified on the drive specified.

Install RBS on the DB and Web/Application Servers

The RBS bits need to be installed on the database server and on each Web server and Application server that exist in the Share-Point farm. The RBS bits are a separate installation as part of the SQL Server 2012 Feature Pack.

Scroll down on the feature pack download page and locate the RBS download:

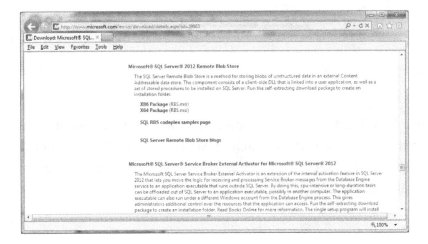

Download the appropriate package (hopefully x64) and save it in a central location.

For the first web server (or database server), create a new batch file, in the same location as you downloaded RBS.msi, using the following code (all on one line - no line breaks):

msiexec /qn /lvx* rbs_install_log.txt /i RBS.msi

TRUSTSERVERCERTIFICATE=true FILEGROUP=PRIMARY
DBNAME="<ContentDbName>"
DBINSTANCE="<DBInstanceName>"
FILESTREAMFILEGROUP=RBSFilestreamProvider
FILESTREAMSTORENAME=FileStreamStore

Open a Command Prompt and execute the first batch file:

Verify success by reviewing the rbs_install_log.txt file that was generated in the same folder. The completion message is not the very last thing but it is towards the end of the log:

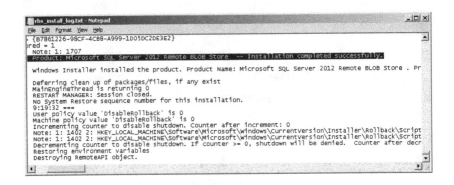

On all of the other web servers and application servers, place the following code into a batch file (again no line breaks):

msiexec /qn /lvx* rbs_install_log.txt /i RBS.msi DBNAME="ContentDbName" DBINSTANCE="DBInstanceName" ADDLOCAL="Client,Docs,Maintainer,ServerScript,FilestreamClient, FilestreamServer"

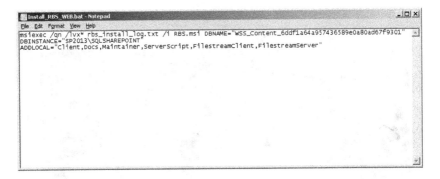

Open a Command Prompt and execute the second batch file on each web server and application server:

```
C:\ Administrator: C:\Windows\system32\cmd.exe - Install_RBS_Web                    _ |□| x|

Y:\spblob>dir
 Volume in drive Y is Data
 Volume Serial Number is DEC1-B9DE

 Directory of Y:\spblob

07/24/2012  09:23 AM    <DIR>          .
07/24/2012  09:23 AM    <DIR>          ..
07/24/2012  09:18 AM               260 Install_RBS_SQL.bat
07/24/2012  09:23 AM               217 Install_RBS_WEB.bat
07/24/2012  09:06 AM         5,242,880 RBS.msi
07/24/2012  09:19 AM         1,424,736 rbs_install_log.txt
               4 File(s)      6,668,093 bytes
               2 Dir(s)  37,603,364,864 bytes free

Y:\spblob>Install_RBS_Web

Y:\spblob>msiexec /qn /lvx* rbs_install_log.txt /i RBS.msi DBNAME="WSS_Content_6
ddf1a64a957436589e0a80ad67f9301" DBINSTANCE="SP2013\SQLSHAREPOINT" ADDLOCAL="Cli
ent,Docs,Maintainer,ServerScript,FilestreamClient,FilestreamServer"
_
```

Enable RBS on the Content Database

To enable RBS on the content database, you must use PowerShell. Therefore, open up PowerShell or Notepad and create the following PowerShell Script:

```
$cdb = Get-SPContentDatabase -
WebApplication "<Web Application Name>"
$rbss = $cdb.RemoteBlobStorageSettings
$rbss.Installed()
$rbss.Enable()
$rbss.SetActiveProviderName($rbss.GetProviderNames()[0])
$rbss
```

You may also add $rbss.MinimumBlobStorageSize=1048576 to increase the minimum file size that will be considered for RBS. The example number shows 1MB.

```
Enable_RBS.ps1 - Notepad
File  Edit  Format  View  Help
$cdb = Get-SPContentDatabase -WebApplication "SharePoint - 80"
$rbss = $cdb.RemoteBlobStorageSettings
$rbss.Installed()
$rbss.Enable()
$rbss.SetActiveProviderName($rbss.GetProviderNames()[0])
$rbss
```

Save the script as a .ps1 file and then open the SharePoint 2013
Management Shell:

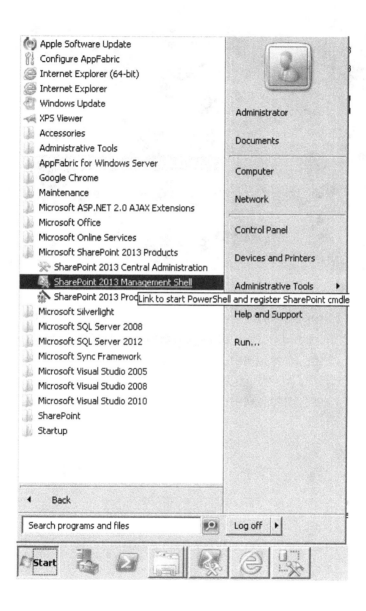

Execute the script:

```
Administrator: SharePoint 2013 Management Shell                          _ |□| x|
PS Y:\spblob> dir

    Directory: Y:\spblob

Mode                LastWriteTime     Length Name
----                -------------     ------ ----
-a---          7/24/2012   9:48 AM        204 Enable_RBS.ps1
-a---          7/24/2012   9:18 AM        260 Install_RBS_SQL.bat
-a---          7/24/2012   9:23 AM        217 Install_RBS_WEB.bat
-a---          7/24/2012   9:06 AM    5242880 RBS.msi
-a---          7/24/2012   9:24 AM     578926 rbs_install_log.txt

PS Y:\spblob> .\Enable_RBS.ps1
True

        Enabled ActiveProviderName  MinimumBlobStorageS UpgradedPersistedPr
                                                    ize operties
        ------- ------------------  ------------------- -------------------
           True FilestreamStore                       0 {}

PS Y:\spblob> _
```

The first output is "True" which means RBS has been installed correctly. The second output displays the RemoteBlobStorageSettings object and shows that RBS is enabled and displays the name of the Active Provider (which should be the same name you used as the FILESTREAMSTORENAME in the RBS installation batch file.

Test RBS

Now it's time to see this working in action! Navigate to your SharePoint site related to the content database you just config-ured. Open a document library:

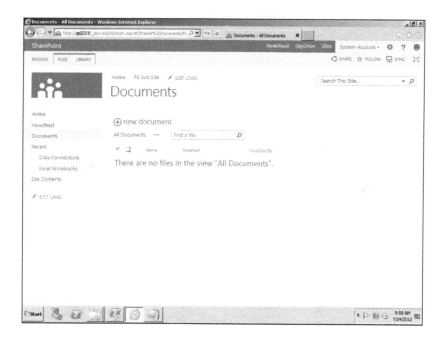

Upload a bunch of documents into the document library:

Investigate the folders within the local file system blob storage location:

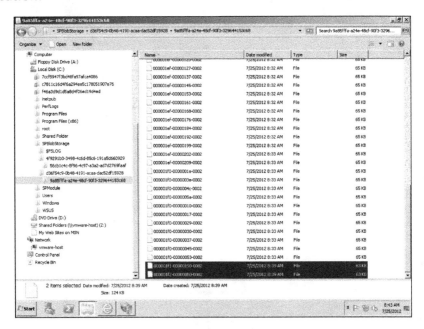

Files appear in small chunks. They will not be human readable.

About the Author

Steve Mann was born and raised in Philadelphia, Pennsylvania, where he still resides. He is an Enterprise Application Engineer for Morgan Lewis and has over 20 years of professional experience. He has authored and co-authored several books related to collaboration technology. Steve graduated Drexel University in 1993.

Steve's blog site can be found at: www.SteveTheManMann.com

Follow Steve on Twitter @stevethemanmann